On the Prowl with Lawrence

by
Margaret Woodhouse

LEARNING · DEVELOPMENT · AIDS

LDA

First published 1990

LDA
Duke Street, Wisbech, Cambs. PE13 2AE

LD 959
ISBN 1-85503-086-1 Paperback
ISBN 1-85503-093-4 Hardback

Created and designed by Magari Publishing, PO Box 74 266, Auckland New Zealand.
Printed and bound in New Zealand by Interprint Printing.

Lawrence is a Praying Mantis who'll surprise you!
He is a chap who'll shock the socks off any fly who...

...zips past unsuspectingly.

He is LONG, and he is GREEN with great WINGS that sweep down his back. His two legs he holds up under his CHIN. And what a chin! Large and chompy and...

...perfect to gobble his food with!

He has a HEAD which is ve-ry small. But on top
of it he has two huge bulging EYES. He can turn
his head this way...

And right around that way to use his eyes to...

...spy on tasty morsels that stray his way!

He even has two EARS. They are the most extraordinary ears you will ever see, tucked into the sides of his front legs. They are a bright purple and they shine in the sun when he walks. When he listens very hard he can hear even the smallest mayfly approach...

...and flit right into his grasp!

His LEGS are awfully long. He has six altogether.
Both of his front legs have spines running down
them. Lawrence uses these like a fork to make it
easier for him to...

...munch
and crunch
his food with!

With his back four legs he...

...moves...

...across...

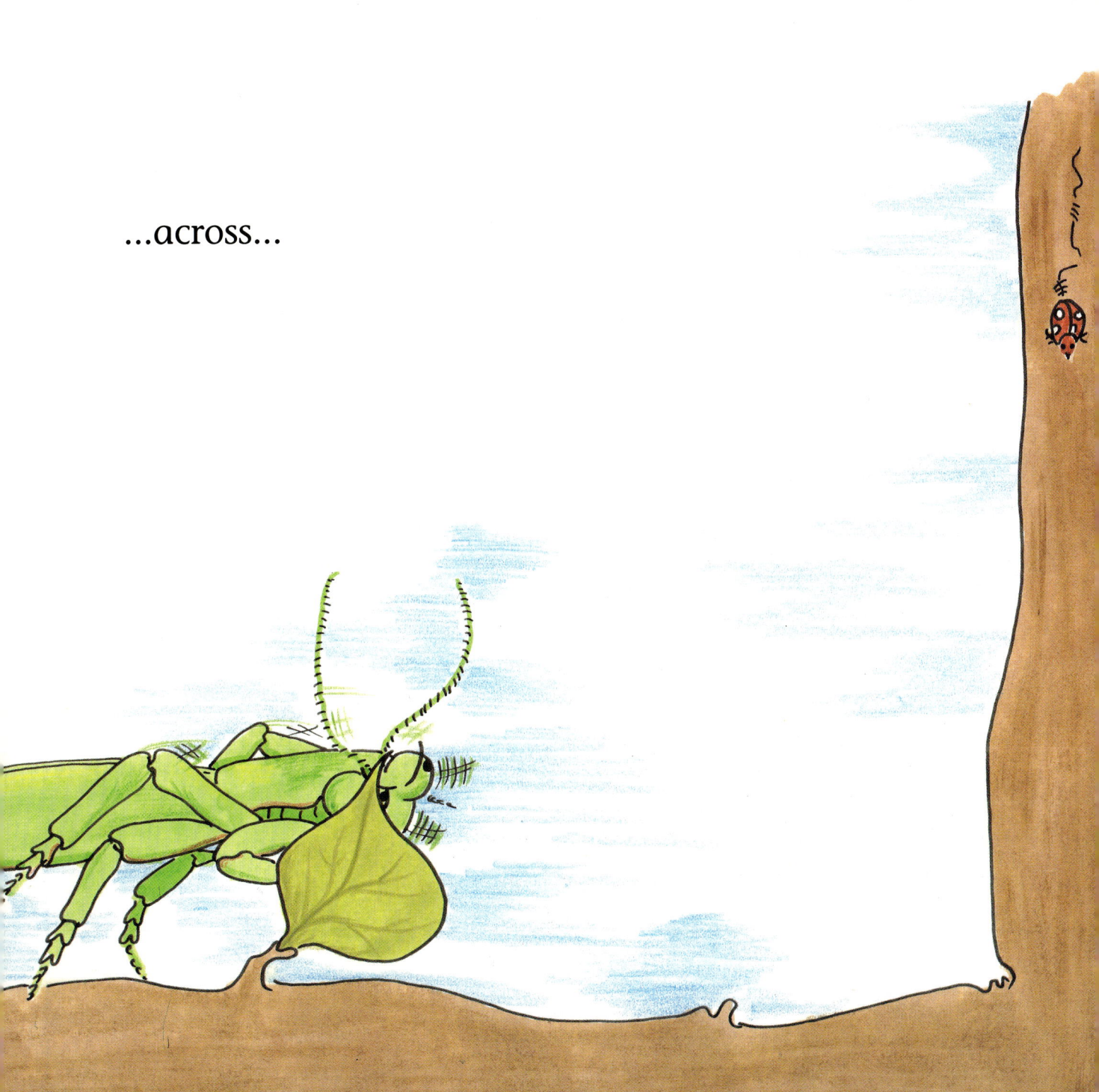

...the leaves...

…to…

...pounce on his next victim!

But don't go getting the wrong idea about Lawrence.

He's quite a charming fellow - really.